A Gentle Call—Come

Poems and Psalms

CHERYL LYN WYNN

Inspiring Voices®

A Service of **Guideposts**

Inspiring Voices books may be ordered through booksellers or by contacting:

Inspiring Voices
1663 Liberty Drive
Bloomington, IN 47403
www.inspiringvoices.com
1 (866) 697-5313

Scripture taken from the King James Version of the Bible.

ISBN: 978-1-4624-0818-4 (sc)
ISBN: 978-1-4624-0817-7 (e)

Library of Congress Control Number: 2013919833

Printed in the United States of America.

Inspiring Voices rev. date: 11/05/2013

CONTENTS

This book could not have been written without positive inspiration from many.

My Pastor, Jonathan Wiggins and his wife Amy from Resurrection Fellowship have given me great encouragement. The atmosphere that is created is that of great love. God's presence falls and permeates our spirits, hearts and minds. We as a church are encouraged to know that with God all things are possible. Nothing is more special than the Bible because it works. The Word of God is powerful. We must maintain a sensitivity to the Holy Spirit. I can do all things through Christ who gives me strength. The most important is that the love of God imparts our soul and His love is the filling that makes us whole. The world will know us by God's love. We must praise God in the time of adversity because praise confuses our enemies. My name is really now not my name because God has changed my name as I am known on earth. I am really now just an impostor. God heals. Miracles are for this day and always. Take a deep breath. Love, live and praise! But the most important is to love.

My daughter Robyn is a great inspiration. She writes me notes and is an enduring encourager. We must find the positive in every situation. When God closes one door another door is opened. My granddaughter, Taryn is always on the sideline to cheer me on.

My son, Philip listens and gives me great counsel. He is a man of honor. I admire all he has done in his life and for our country. He and his wife Sook have been a great support for me in my life and I am grateful we have one another. Jake, their son warms my spirit and makes my heart smile.

My friends and family are a great advocate. My brother Michael and I talk on the telephone analyzing our great life adventures. Some of the pictures came from my Grandmother and Grandfather's yard in their honor. Friends listen and I listen. Friends are just gifts from God that are like frosting and ice cream on a cake. You can never have enough friends, family or ice cream.

My God is ever faithful and oh so near. I could not write without His small voice revealing at times what word shall be written next. God sent His Son, Jesus to shed His blood and die for me and you too. I sense the great presence of The Holy Spirit leading me each and every day. He fills my heart with such joy.

This could not be complete without a written honor of the other pastors at Resurrection Fellowship and, I cannot mention them all. Pastor Bill Kline and his wife Deborah prayed over my hearing loss. Pastor Bill sang great words of healing. Pastor Diane Blanco is our prayer pastor and is a great encouragement to me. Her smile, her strength and her great insight is an honor to acclaim. Pastor Kathy Melson is just so fun! She shares from the depth of her heart and conveys warmth and reality.

I thank all of my great encouragers that are in my life. I thank God for blessings abundantly.

And God - can you please restore my hearing? Thank you.

COME...

Matthew 11: 28-30 (KJV)
"COME unto me, all ye that labour and are
heavy laden and I will give you rest."
"Take my yoke upon you, and learn of me; for I am
meek and lowly in heart: and ye shall find rest unto your
souls. For my yoke is easy, and my burden is light."

FREEDOM

I pledge allegiance to my Christ who for me lived and died;
Under one nation we do live: in corporate implied.
The Tower of Babel fell with many languages spoke:
Traditions and ideas became, un-understood; broke.
Fighting and consternation of ideas strong and bold;
Created diversity in men of ages young and old.
Now nations rise against nations causing distress and war...
Instead of living together on earth, unity we must restore.
Families are broken, loved ones away with peace to possibly find...
Fighting battles that cannot be won; it's Satan we need to bind.
Bow before our God and King; open our hearts for one another care;
Honor those that are deployed or home alone, pray their lives to spare.
Open your heart daily down on bended knee.
Ask Jesus Christ to enter in and allow your heart to see...
How can I make a difference to one each and every day?
I must help others even in diversity for Christ; He His blood did pay...
My debt, for my life and gave me strength to do just as I must;
I have the resurrection power living alive within my spirit - trust.
As I pledge allegiance to my Christ who for me died;
The pain that He did suffer and the Words that He cried.
We will never be forsaken and we'll never be alone.
Jesus Christ made a promise that someday we will go home...
Where we will live for eternity and all will be as one.
Right now on this earth together we need to strive to see the SON.
Pray for our warriors that fight our battle foe;
Petitioning for them daily that angels bestow...
Presence and protection in a war that should not be.
We all just need to realize that Jesus died and we are in Him free.

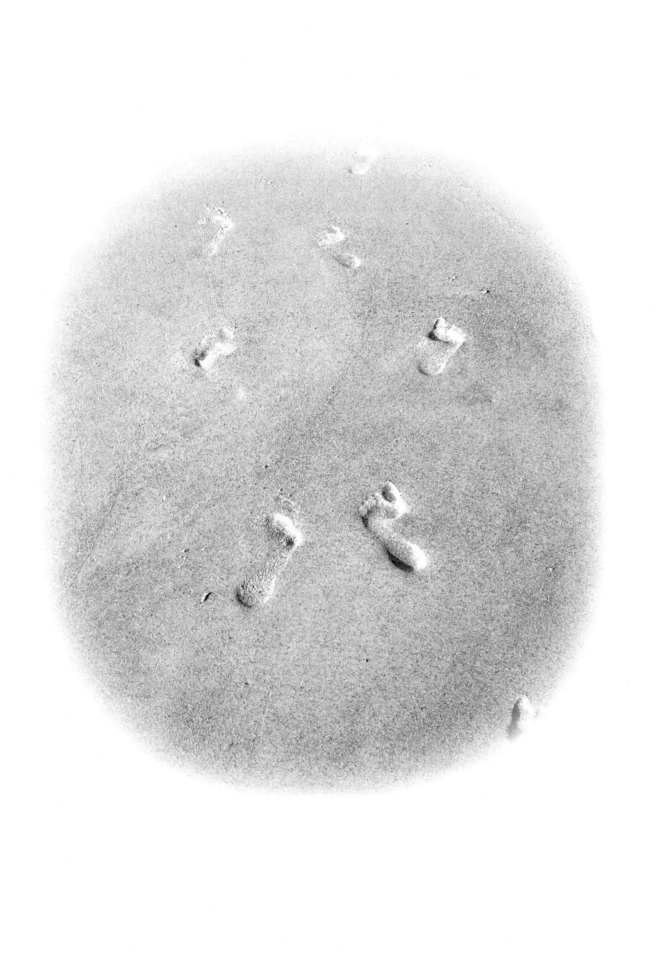

TIME

Time did not exist before God spoke time into being;
Eternity's trail fleeing...
Each existence created an image: a you and a me;
To be alive, to create a life, perfectly.
A beginning of a script, an appearance; a first breath...
Drawn to be written, a story hath saith.
A book with a start but no end in sight;
You are the author of you; the conclusion you must write.
Carefully and deliberately with each passing word;
Each second in life doth move end-ward.
Many choices will come along the way;
The weight of decisions in what one may do or might say...
Will make all the difference in life and how it will end;
So in the beginning the footprints along life's path extend...
To millions of steps encased in time;
To a conclusion that is unknown; sublime.
The last chapter is written and the end proclaimed;
The book is finished...a memory named.

PSALM 81:9-12 (KJV)

"There shall no strange god be in thee; neither
shalt thou worship any strange god."

"I AM the Lord they God, which brought thee out of the
land of Egypt: open thy mouth wide and I will fill it."

"But my people would not hearken to my
voice; and Israel would not of me."

"So I gave them up unto their own hearts' lust:
and they walked in their own counsels."

I AM

Come with Me and learn to live...
Freely, by grace I will give.
Are you thirsty and tired? I will renew...
Give you drink, It's ME, I AM waiting for you.
Worship, worship in spirit and in truth, desire...
To worship; Jesus Christ I AM your fire.
I long for a relationship, your love I do yearn;
I AM Jesus Christ, I'll quench your soul, do discern.
Come let Me heal you, come let Me love;
Trust ME, I AM Jesus as gentle as a dove.
MY arms will embrace you, MY love doth restore...
Your life and your spirit, heaven implore.
Pray for it all: both the big and the small;
Forgive the little, forgive it all.
I love you more than all the grains of sand;
I love you my children, I'll take your hand.
Instead of condemnation I'll understand...
I'll show you love without demand.
I wish to be your friend on earth.
I want to give your life new birth.

You are Holy, my God, You are my friend.
I accept you as my Savior keep my life until the end.
I want to follow You, I cry out Your Holy Name.
Jesus Christ please heal me, please keep me as I remain.
This day is fashioned just for me alone.
I know that you will provide for me, You promised to atone...
Grace and mercy, trust and love;
My advocate for me now above.
You've changed my name to beloved and friend.
I will love you Oh Jesus forever, AMEN.

Psalm 105:4 (KJV)

"Seek the Lord, and His strength: Seek His face evermore."

A GENTLE BLOWING WIND

I was blind but now I see;
The wonders of Thy majesty.
I could not taste or could not smell;
The gloriousness for-tell.
I could not hear the blowing wind;
The rush the earth somehow didst amend.
I could not feel; my heart stood still;
A stillness my spirit and soul didst fill.

I miraculously turned and found;
A beaconing, calling sound.
Come, Follow ME until the end;
I will be your forever friend.

I began to feel the wind,
Gently blowing: it did descend…
Upon my soul and into my heart;
The scent of something did impart.
I saw the light and wonders as it brightly shone;
I sensed this led me somewhere, somewhere that I should roam.
My heart did open, my spirit accepted this kind and gentle man.
My taste grew sweet and I could hear the sound of a *amen*.
As I looked up the light shown; brightly on my head;
I suddenly realized a peace and knew I had nothing now to dread.

I could see the wonders of all the majesty He did create;
The rushing sounds of silence from the earth was no longer now my fate.
The miracle and the marvel that caused me to hear His voice;
Is alive and living in my heart and causing me now to rejoice.

Psalm 107:19 (KJV)

"Then they cry unto the Lord in their trouble, and
He saveth them out of their distress."

TRUST

I'm sorry Lord for sinning, for turning my back away.

Oh Jesus Christ come in my heart and with me always stay.

Please don't ever leave me and each day my life to fill…

Fill me with your Holy Spirit and cause me to do your will.

Each day I will spend time with you and give you all my life.

Thank you Lord for delivering me and taking all my strife.

Thank you Jesus for dying on the cross with outstretched hands.

Thank you also for loving me, I trust in your commands.

I thank you Jesus for daily life and being with me now.

I believe in what you've said and done, my heart I humbly bow.

AMEN

Psalm 107:20 (KJV)

"He sent His Word, and healed them, and
delivered them from their destruction."

SALVATION PROCLAIM

Come to me, into my arms and sing a different song;
A song about our great God to whom we do belong.
Sing for joy and for thanksgiving, hold your banner high.
Praise and adoration for the Lord, my King…I;
I will bless His name forever, salvation to proclaim.
Splendor and majesty ascribe His Holy Name.
Holy, Holy, Holy is the Lord on high.
Holy, Holy, Holy wickedness defy.
Break forth and sing His praises, shout before the mighty King…
Praises to the Lord doth my spirit sing.
Worship at His feet down on bended knee.
Enter into His gates and you will truly see…
His everlasting loving kindness and His bountiful grace;
In His precious presence you will clearly see His face.
Come into my blessedness and spend some time with me;
I will hold you in my arms and set your spirit free.

Psalm 103:17 (KJV)

"But the mercy of the Lord is from everlasting to everlasting. Upon them that fear Him, and His righteousness unto children's children."

SCATTER MY ENEMIES

Oh Lord my adversaries have increased this very day;
Please Oh Lord protect me from getting in harms way.
Thou Oh Lord are a shield in and out;
Warring angels, armed heavily about.
With fetters of iron Thine enemy cords are cast...
Away - far away in the past.
May the enemy be like the chaff of the wind...
Picked up and scattered; incompetent descend.
No evil will dwell; no vile will stand;
Your abundant love wilt take command.
The wicked will be destroyed: arise and attack;
My enemies wilt all in weakness fall back.
Execute judgment: cause a snare to drop down;
Rain fire and brimstone in your wind blown.
Enemies consumed, empty them out as mire.
Cause devastation in their camp; inspire...
By your voice the wilderness doth cause to shake;
Under the enemy's feet doth quake.
I trust in you Lord, make my face to shine.
Hide me in Thy secret place from man's conspired design.
The eye of the Lord is on he who doth fear,
In your loving kindness keep me alive and so near.
Command victories over adversaries: trampled, cause them shame.
We surrender in gratitude and glory to your HOLY NAME.

Psalm 72:6 (KJV)

"He shall come down like rain upon the mown grass, as showers that water the earth."

RAIN ANEW

Enter in to the fragrance of Jesus Christ our King;
You will connect with the odor of manifesting.
Jesus is perfect in all He did live;
Calming storms, healing and authority give.
Revelation in Christ in miracles raised;
The power from within wants out, always.
Like a river that flows in the nature of God;
Rise oh rise where saints have trod.
Ponder in the mind to be taught… to fashion;
The canvas in which to paint… passion.
Renew my mind, my soul to an encounter divine;
Oh Lord Jesus flow, give me experience sublime.
Cause me to step out in your presence and your might;
Giving to others … impart new insight.
Cause me not to dwell on what has happened … not.
Count on prophecy, yearning destiny anew… sought.
Transform my life to be who I am;
Create in me Lord within my inner man.
Enter in to the fragrance of the King.
Wear it, accept it and allow the essence to bring…
The kingdom of heaven to rain on my soul;
In gentle perfection Jesus will fully make me whole.

WHOLENESS

God loves us as two parents searching in the night;
For a lost and wandering child... alone and full of fright.
God has opened up His arms; He died for you and me.
He stands at the door and knocks... waiting for us to be.
He will give you life and freedom and forgive you of every sin.
Behold the Christ who died for you and wants to take you in.
Listen to the voice of God... His voice is very clear.
Open up your heart... allow Him to calm all fear.
We can then sit down with Him and at the Father's throne;
Hear the Holy Spirit in your inner being alone.
Come to Christ in expectation for He will redeem your soul.
It is thru Jesus and His great love that you will be made whole.

Psalm 143:10 (KJV)

"Teach me to do Thy will; for Thou art my God: Thy
spirit is good; lead me into the land of uprightness."

TIME IS CHANGE

Being has no beginning or being has no end.
Human kind-ness is difficult to comprehend.
To understand life is the experience of living;
Loving, desiring, wealth and giving.
A blind man does not know darkness he cannot see;
Nor, can he see light, the world: visually.
We were created and create, we are thought in our mind…
We are life flowing on earth, gentle and kind.
Made of relationships, our bodies are part…
Experiencing change is time…start.
To learn and to know how to heal within;
Regenerating again and again.
Imbalance causes issues we cannot see;
The body is healthy when the mind is free.
Changing with rhythms: an unending beat…
Awake and asleep, dancing feet.
Any sensory input to our mind makes a change;
The rhythm of life is then rearranged.
Ourselves we can vary, not others, their intent…
Background noise of judgment stills…resent?
Being stuck in a possibility is held…
Committing our selves to prison, dispelled.
There is no existence that was not first a notion.
Knowledge, the non-attached witness that animates motion.
The unknown is the field of possibilities - dream…
Our mind: planning…thinking a scheme.
Interpreting feelings and understanding life,

Living daily, contentment and strife.
In just being, we are created and free;
The choices we make allow us to be.
Reality, life, pleasures and pain...
Life flows - again and again.
Moving and growing, creating a beat;
Rhythm, each moment, success and defeat.
Respect uniqueness, respond from within;
Signals effect, in mind...begin.
To wonder, to ponder, to seek and to find...
Our bodies are changing...mind.
Flowing thoughts, feeling, hearing, seeing...still;
Changing life effects until...
Life flowing doth stop...

Beginning anew...
No e n d . . . eternity is due.

Time is change flowing through life...
Each day we live: pleasure and strife.
Born to live...live to die:
Living life, the question is why?
We do, we speak, we believe and we feel...
Compassion flowing, life is real.
Balance inspired, greatness obtained...
Through peace and living life is gained.

RELATIONSHIP

We are a door unto our lives, a way of which to find…
Confidence and the love of Christ; of Christ's mind.
Walking through an open door what will you behold?
A newness in life in a moment; a life untold.
A movement rising: an awakening of spirit be;
Come away and walk through the open door and see.
Encounter Christ, a blessing that will set you free;
Oh Holy Spirit, come unto me.
God's intent is never to be carried by man…
On a bed of rules made by man's plan.
Religion enters in and causes death.
Christ is alive and desires our each and every breath.
God will subdue mine enemies and cause them to depart.
He claims my life, my spirit and enters in my heart.
Invade in to intimacy: God's stronghold and desires;
I need the Holy Spirit to fall, please inspire…
My heart, my life, my mind each moment and each day.
My own understanding I trust to Christ, I pray.
Penetrate my spirit and cause your ways to permeate my mind;
A flavor of You, Holy Spirit in my being prompt me to find.
Your kingdom come upon my life, You are truly real.
Wholeness fall, newness come and instruct my heart to feel.
I am a door, a gateway to life and love and desire to be free…
My heart is filled with Christ allowing me to be.
He will enter in my kingdom … now will come…
In Christ is our each moment as each instant hath begun.
Enter in unto the door and in our life will find…
The love of Christ consume me and behold me in my mind.

Psalm 27:1 (KJV)

"The Lord is my light and my salvation; whom shall I fear?
The Lord is the strength of my life, of whom shall I be afraid?"

EMBRACE GOD'S PRESENCE

I learned to love not wide but deep…
Into the soul where love doth seep:
Life's ebb and flow doth not despair,
When our heart is blessed, God doth care.
Share each moment…each breath…each day.
Blessings poured out, blessings repay.
Striving with each passing step we take;
Love is real, love is right, love is not fake.
Pour out hatred, resentment and pride.
Apprehend love for your life to fill and reside.
Seek the Son, His presence will satiate with grace.
God's existence will bless, your heart embrace.
Reach out, reach deep into each new dawn.
Seek love: pour blessings within and upon.
Each living soul that yet has breath…
Praise God! Find love until death.
It's then He'll open … His arms ascend…
To you He will speak, "Welcome home my friend."
Received into eternity, this day to you will belong…
Blessings will flow…you'll find in your soul a new song.

Psalm 86:6-8 (KJV)

"Give ear, O Lord, unto my prayer; and attend
to the voice of my supplications."

"In the day of my trouble I will call upon thee: for thou wilt answer me."

"Among the gods there is none like unto thee, O Lord;
neither are there any works like unto thy works."

BE YE WHOLE

It is your faith that has made you whole;
Come unto me, your spirit and soul…
Illness…isolation…clothed in aloneness;
Draw nigh and be rescued by holiness.
The veil rent doth permeate…
Jesus came and sealed my fate.
When the presence of the Lord falls we change;
Our spirit is touched: rearranged.
Lift up your voices in unity cry…
Press in to Jesus - do not defy.
Jesus can heal, save, doth deliver;
Power personified, passion giver.
Do not give up just rise and enter…
Into conviction believe: gather…
In childlike faith be still and come.
Come unto Jesus, He's calling you, come.

UNBOUNDEDNESS

Bondage in life holds us stuck in time;
In a prison, conditions confine.
In boundaries that will not allow me to be…
Who I am alive and free.

Reality is a perception, a notion.
The source of a thought, explosion…
An opinion then, reality becomes real;
A shape, an event you can see and feel.

Freedom comes from understanding opposites like joy and sorrow;
Discerning can produce tomorrow…
What we think and feel and know and see…
Reflect: reconcile to self quietly.

We must have the knowledge to step into the unknown;
Break loose from the shackles that life has sown.
Release fear of the future, attain harmony and joy.
A new world is birthed…employ.

Infinite and eternal, un-bounded-ness in mind;
Transcended by thought, pure and kind.
Simple and balanced, aware and true.
Live life and give birth in all that you do.

Psalm 142:7 (KJV)

"Bring my soul out of prison, that I may praise
Thy name: The righteous shall compass me about;
for thou shalt deal bountifully with me."

MARCH FORTH

What must I bury to go on with the Lord?
Give up and put behind life, face heaven-ward.
March forth into Zion with a sword and a stone…
Giants to face, I am not alone.
Grace will shine forth to lead the way…
Mercy and peace will cause my heart to obey.
Blessings will flow in a path like the sea;
Leading me onward to Christ, to be.
In His arms, in His glory my face will shine.
My soul and my spirit, the earth resign.
Demons and life will attempt to ponder…
Causing my direction to wander.
But my eyes are on Christ and my heart is at home;
Keeping my life course, I will not roam.
With the sword in my heart and a stone in my hand…
Giants will flee at my voice command.
Taking authority over the earth and its powers;
Walking with Christ daily, every hour…
Every minute, every second to battle I'll go;
Seeds of blessings and love to Him I will sow.
To Zion I'll march with a sword and a stone.
With Christ in my heart, He will lead me home.

Psalm 141:2 (KJV)

"Let my prayer be set forth before Thee as incense; and
the lifting up of my hands as the evening sacrifice."

Psalm 132:8 (KJV)

"Arise, O Lord, into thy rest; Thou, and the ark of Thy strength."

JUST ONE STEP

We are led in life one step at a time;
In part not the whole does God define.
Take one step by faith and begin another...
In obedience and trust in life to gather.
To seek instruction and His desire:
Direction for the future, require.
Let go of the past, repent and progress;
Receive God's forgiveness and life's best.
Move in God's time and God's perfect will.
Sometimes we must wait and pray, "Peace be still."
The spirit of God will speak commands;
Our heart and mind will understand.
Take one step out and begin anew...
His light will shine ahead of you.
If we never move the light won't be ahead;
Our mind and spirit and soul avoids being fed.
Stagnation and error will fill our lives;
No peace - discontentment, despise.
Listen and hear, God is speaking and knows;
In our heart and mind the Holy Spirit sows...
Kindness and truth and wisdom and life,
He leads us daily in peace and strife.
Take one step out and light your world.
Christ will lead your life, your life unfurled.

Psalm 119:33-34, 41 (KJV)

"Teach me, O Lord, the way of Thy statutes;
and I shall keep it unto the end."

"Give me understanding, and I shall keep Thy law;
yea, I shall observe it with my whole heart."

"Let Thy mercies come also unto me, O Lord, even
Thy salvation, according to Your Word."

A GREATER LOVE

Thank you for the blessings that you have given me.
Love from others that doth allow me to truly see…
The width and depth of your great love and who You truly are.
Come into my life and guide me to the bright and morning star.
Lead me to the manger and guide me to the cross;
Where your precious blood was shed, it was not counted loss.
Your shed blood gives me protection daily from the storm.
Your heart reaches down and touches me and protects me from all harm.
Thank you Lord for dying and for giving my spirit life.
Staying right beside me in happiness and strife.
It's my desire to honor You in all I do and all I am within.
Lord Jesus now be with me and convict me of all sin.
Bless me with your presence and your omnipresent love.
Allow my heart to be assured that someday I'll be above…
High up in the heavens with you in your ever present care.
Until then please never leave me, my life with You I want to share;
The blessings and the glory of life down here on earth.
Anoint me with your affection and give my spirit birth;
To reach out to others and fill them with your love…
So then some day in heaven we'll be together: up above.

Psalm 24:10 (KJV)

"Who is this King of glory?
The Lord of hosts, He is the King of glory."

FRESH MORNING BREEZE

The morning breeze has secrets to tell...
A miracle inspired; for-tell.
Open daily the gift God has prepared for you;
The morning sun with a kiss of dew.
Sweet soft winds that blow delight;
They stir our spirits with His might.
Each morning we sing a good morning song;
The melody resides in our spirit...belong.
The past and our sins have been washed away.
New mercies like dew have fallen this day.
Weeping may last but for only a night;
But joy will rise and give new light.
The sun is rising up over the east;
Bringing newness and a fresh peace.
Along with the loving-kindness of the Lord;
Each day He beckons heavenward.
Peace cannot live with unsettlement and evil.
Peace, great peace comes to those who are able...
To cast aside grief and fear that's unsure;
Allow God to replace anew and pure...
In each morning there is breeze that for you doth bestow;

Secrets in life just for you to know.
Do not limit God with your limitations…
Repeating wrong in life creations.
Our actions this day are to emulate God.
Faith by faith our hearts must trod.
Our redeemer lives and in the end;
A day will dawn in newness … spend…
Eternity forever more doth stand;
In Christ's glory we will take His hand.
He will lead us in this new day;
Reveal morning secrets to us I pray.
Help me Lord with each unfading dawn.
Protect my heart and keep it strong.
Keep me close to you I yearn;
While I walk with you, discern…
In the wind that blows each day…
The Holy Spirit in me doth stay.
Filling my spirit and convicting my heart;
With your freshness I do impart…
My life, my heart and my all to you.
Cause the morning breezes to keep me anew.

Psalm 8:1 (KJV)

"Oh Lord our Lord, how excellent is Thy name in all the earth!"

"Who hast set Thy glory above the heavens."

ENLIGHTEN MY HEART

I must get a revelation from the Lord above;
So I may understand Christ and know His precious love.
Given a new enlightening of the end and its time to come;
Everyone will fall and worship and adore the Holy One.
I must find out who Jesus is and what He's done for me.
He came to earth and lived and died to keep me from death: free.
Christ was appointed heir, the radiance of glory and might.
I am in Jesus Christ a joint heir, in His precious light.
Jesus is the image of God in heaven and on earth.
We're created by Him and for Him to give in us new birth.
Christ was raised from the dead and seated to the right;
By the power of almighty God, infinite … delight.
Satan cannot touch Him and many do not comprehend;
That Jesus is the Son of God and is placed in command.
Jesus is the head of the body of the church below.
It's the direct representation of God our Father, His love to us did bestow.
Without the head the body is dead and has no life inside.
It is Christ that gives me life; in me He does abide.
I am a single member of Christ's body above.
All are created differently in Him by His love.
Each are unique members with talents separately given.
You are called for a special time, anointed, empowered from heaven.
We are members of one body and members of Christ our King, profound…
Satan must now get out, in Christ joint heirs we're found.
We need all the parts of our body to function now as one.
Our hearts must be filled with Christ Jesus, God's only Son.
He will keep you till the end when He returns to take us home at last.
He'll keep us safe and give us life that seems to happen fast.
The Holy Spirit lives within us, with God we are one with Christ above.
Revelation and enlightening fall upon us in His love.

Psalm 23:1 (KJV)

"The Lord is my shepherd. I shall not want."

RESIDE

Wait upon Christ to manifest His will;
There is hope, He is love, peace be still.
The riches of His glory is the inheritance to the saints below.
Our suffering will not compare to the glory we will know.
We are the redeemed of the Lord and in His strength and in His might...
All power in heaven is given to me in His precious sight.
I am an heir of God, all riches belong...
To me, I'm a child of the King, I am strong...
In His power, His might, His majesty and love;
My God, He doth reign, He lives above.
He brings light from the mystery hidden in ages;
The manifold wisdom of God in the pages...
Of time with the rulers and authorities in heavenly places.
Boldness and confidence access faith and graces.
Loose not heart in tribulation on now this earth.
Bow your knees before the Father: birth...
To be strengthened with power through His Spirit and Son;
Christ will dwell in you and with Him make you one.
Exceedingly, abundantly, beyond all that we ask or think;
The power that works within will not allow us to sink.
He'll send ministering angels to be by our side.
But to His children on earth He will speak, reside...
Reside with me in heaven at my right hand.
He will keep us near, till the very end.
Until that day we must trust and obey.
Seeking and hearing what Christ doth say.
In blessed hope, blessed peace and all blessings from above...
Work together for good to those God doth love.
In His hand He doth hold us and in our hearts He doth reside.
In Christ is my confidence and in Him I abide.

Psalm 23:3 (KJV)

"He restoreth my soul; He leadeth me in the paths
of righteousness for His name's sake."

THE REFLECTION OF HEAVEN

The glory of God falls down from above;
He desires our heart to be filled with his love.
In the knowledge of God and the glory of the Lord;
I am changed, my life is heavenward.
A revelation of what the image of Christ conceives;
Creates in our lives an understanding, believes...
The fullness and beauty that shall fall on our heart;
Christ and His love to my life impart.
His glory is broad without beginning or end.
Who am I in His creation if He calls me His friend?
He created many but none are ever the same.
Oh, Holy Spirit in me remain.
Cause your endless love to encompass my life;
In Christ I am, in both stillness and strife.
The heavens declare the glory of God...
I praise you Oh Lord, my heart doth trod...
To march to the beat of your pulse above.
Oh God, you created this all with your love.
In you and your name cause my spirit to proclaim;
Mercy and grace, your majesty sustain.
The reflection of your SON; and what I do see,
Will cause me to live and cause me to be...
In your holiness, your presence, your wisdom from above;
Forbearing, forgiving in kindness and love.
Envelop my spirit with strength, truth and might.
Cause me to care for others...delight.
Cast away sin and may evil have no control.
In my life You will extinguish flaming darts aimed at my soul.
With prayer and thanksgiving all evil must leave.
Please stay forever in my spirit, cleave.
Into the likeness of Christ that I now see;
May others truly discern His reflection in me.

Psalm 29:11 (KJV)

"The Lord will give strength unto His people, the
Lord will bless His people with peace."

MERCIES TENDER

Drought, death, disease, disaster spoke;
God's love revoke?
Hidden riches in secret places;
Small clouds creating spaces.
Disaster falls and causes strife;
Undeniable measure…life.
To stir our hope, adversity doth come;
Undo as we know - begun.
Nothing is impossible with God above.
Come to the water - receive His love.
Stir our reality: create anew;
Come Holy Spirit - renew…
Revive my life, my heart, my soul;
Create in my being…make me whole.
The drought in life will begin to flood.
My spirit is drenched with Jesus' blood.
Death no longer has its sting.
In Christ we live, in Him we sing.
Disease has lost the power to be;
My body is whole, I am set free.
Salvation hath come with mercy: tender;
To Christ my King I do surrender.

Psalm 142:3 (KJV)

"When my spirit was overwhelmed within me,
then Thou knowest my path..."

Psalm 93:4 (KJV)

"The Lord on high is mightier than the noise of many
waters, yea, than the mighty waves of the sea."

FINAL VICTORY

My feet are guided into peace: the way;
To shine upon those who in darkness stay.
Being delivered from the enemy's hand;
Serve Christ without fear, command.
Give to others the knowledge of salvation, be;
Forgiveness of sin, we are set free.
By Jesus' blood that was shed for you;
Tender mercies of God will make each new.
His Spirit is given without measure…our mind…
Cannot conceive His love…defined.
It reaches as far as the east is to the west;
In our spirit His love doth desire to rest.
COME to Christ Jesus and in Him live;
The final victory He will give.
My spirit, my soul, my heart wilt shine;
I will forever be His and Jesus will forever be mine.

Psalm 25:4 (KJV)

"Show me Thy ways, O Lord; teach me Thy paths."

GLORIOUS LIGHT

Peace, peace, God's peace…flow down from the heavens above.
The more I surrender the less I'm consumed, the more my heart doth love.
I praise you Lord my Father, for your glorious light.
Help me not focus on my circumstances, cause me to delight…
In your strength and in your will and what you've done for me.
Each day cause me to become more secure in your peace and tranquility.
You shed your blood upon the cross; holy, blameless and true…
Cause my eyes to open and my heart to seek anew.
Transcend me with understanding and fill my heart with truth and grace.
Let my foundation not be shaken, keep my eyes upon your face.
Give me precious peace, in times of great despair.
Always help me comprehend that I stay in your care.
Know when infirmities and troubles appear to me as strife;
You stand alert and ready to establish peace and life.
I must learn to lay down the problems that I daily face.
I must know you are my God of hope, my amazing grace.
My understanding shall remain steadfast, not anxious, giving thanks and praise.
The peace of God will guard my heart and mind for all my days.

MAY GOD'S PEACE FILL YOUR LIFE.

PSALM 7:1 KJV

"O Lord my God, in Thee do I put my trust: save me
from all them that persecute me, and deliver me..."

Psalm 7:17 (KJV)

"I will praise the Lord according to His righteousness: and
will sing praise to the name of the Lord most high."

ALWAYS AND FOREVER

The veil is rent, my heart is free…
Christ Jesus lives, He lives in me.
I've asked Him in, He's come to stay:
He'll never leave, or go away.
He saved my life and cleansed each sin;
By His blood I can live again.
The oil of the Holy Spirit covers my life;
Daily convicted, protected from strife.
Now each night as I lay down to rest,
I pray each day I've done my best.
I pray He's with me as I sleep…
Until I wake my soul He'll keep.
When I stir a new day dawn;
In my heart He'll place a fresh new song.
He'll guide my steps and take my hand;
He'll lead me to the promised land.
He'll give me strength to live each day;
In my heart place words that I must say.
With you I desire to forever reside…
It is in your shadow I desire to hide.
Your power and your love each please fill…
My life, my heart, my peace be still.
Allow me to always know you'll never leave or forsake me;
Through you Oh Lord my life please be.
Permit me to see you and seek your grace…
Always and forever my soul, embrace.

DANCE WITH ME

COME dance, romance and give me a chance;
I loved you so at first glance.
I fell in love the moment you were there…
COME dance with me alone, I care.
You see I came to earth one day;
I came and knew that I had to pay…
The cost of eternal life for you.
COME dance each step, you I pursue.
I will lead if you will follow;
Each step in life below.
I will gently hold your hand;
You will grow to understand…

My Love

It's Jesus, I have been longing you to see. Your heart and soul come dance
with
ME.

Psalm 27:4 (KJV)

"One thing have I desired of the Lord, that will I seek after; that I may dwell in the house of the Lord all the days of my life, to behold the beauty of the Lord, and to inquire in His temple."

UNFASTENED

Let us greet this day that I am assigned;
Which snatches us up in time...confined.
Restoring anew a presence of mind,
In foreign places; combined...
With precepts in the present specifically designed;
For this our day: each moment defined.
A climax of history retains what is done;
While dwelling on earth: time begun.
Mortality begins each day sure;
Life to death is living's cure.
Freedom in being each day behold;
Life ends in an instant...c o l d.
What is your belief; doth your mind comprehend...
At life's end is death a friend?
It unfastens us from earth, a brief stay drawn nigh;
Our bodies are undone...to where must I lie?

Psalm 57:1 (KJV)

"Be merciful unto me, O God, be merciful unto me; for my soul trusteth
in Thee: Yea, in the shadow of Thy wings will I make my refuge..."

THANK YOU LORD

I'm sorry Lord for sinning, for turning my back away.

Oh Jesus Christ come in my heart and with me always stay.

Please don't ever leave me and each day my life to fill…

Fill me with your Holy Spirit and cause me to do Your will.

Each day I will spend time with You and give You all my life.

Thank You Lord for delivering me and taking all my strife.

Thank You Lord for dying on the cross with outstretched hands.

Thank You Lord for loving me, I trust in Your commands.

I thank You Lord for daily life and being with me now.

I believe in what You've said and done, my heart I humbly bow.

Psalm 57:3 (KJV)

"He shall send from heaven, and save me from the
reproach of him that would swallow me up.
God shall send forth His mercy and truth."

POSSIBILITIES

Allow my mind to serve my spirit in me;
By faith in Christ I will truly see.
Burning is rising from within my heart;
In a personal encounter in part.
No unbelief from God is rebuked not;
He is unconcerned about my doubt sought.
Darkness and death is driven out by trust in heart…
The impossible, the life from Christ impart.
All possibilities are in effect, in a seed…
Of belief: of a new beginning breed.
Each step is in faith, each step is in light…
Of the Lord Jesus Christ, His voice insight.
The roots of doubt will whither away.
Christ will enter…faith will stay.
My mind and my spirit in mercy I'll see;
My heart and my soul will be set free.

Psalm 57:5 (KJV)

"Be Thou exalted, O God, above the heavens;

let Thy glory be above all the earth."

LEAD ME TO JESUS

Know truth in my heart and wisdom in my mind;
Come and rest, transformation find.
Behold Jesus Christ, the hope of glory;
In my heart doth create a story.
In His time my heart will sing;
Revealed by Your fire, You are my King.
Lead me to Jesus in wisdom, truth and love.
Read in the Word, reveal heaven above.
O Jesus in this life and all that I will be;
I must come to You and You will set my life free.

Psalm 95:6 (KJV)

"O come, let us worship and bow down: Let us
kneel before the Lord our maker."

KNEEL AND PRAY

My words become sweeter each day;
As I kneel and pray...
Growing close to you Oh Lord,
Moving in life ... heaven ward.

I AM the blood of the Lamb please come.
Access to the throne...run...
Wake up and enter you precious one;
I AM that I AM God's Son.

The best and the worst may fall.
A foundation unshakable to all...
That have come and built their life in my love;
I will keep you in might and power above.

Today heaven has manna to feed.
Blessings doth flow for each need...
Show me this day Your desire for my soul;
Deliver me and keep me whole.

Chase after the kingdom of God to find.
Freedom and righteousness in your mind...
Getting to know You more each day;
As I kneel and pray.

Psalm 119:2 (KJV)

"Blessed are they that keep His testimonies. and
that seek Him with the whole heart."

COME

He gently led me to the gate;
Behold, His glory was my fate.
His voice was like pounding waters … resound…
To hear Him within my heart did pound.
The glory of the Lord didst fall…
Into my inner being: my all.
He knew my name, He knew my heart;
Come He called and ne'er depart.
My spirit did follow this gentle man.
I knew He was the great I AM.
I desire to be with Him, His light doth shine;
In darkness he claimed my heart for Thine.
This earthen vessel is now made whole;
Jesus Christ is alive within my soul.

Come...

Romans 10:13 (KJV)

"For whosoever shall call upon the name of the Lord shall be saved."

Romans 8:38-39 (KJV)

"For I am persuaded, that neither death, nor life, nor angels, nor principalities, nor powers, nor things present, nor things to come, nor height, nor depth, nor any other creature, shall be able to separate us from the love of God, which is in Christ Jesus our Lord."

AMEN

Thank you for spending time with me;
Hearing the call from Christ to be…
Allowing Him to become your friend;
Getting to know Him until the end.
Quiet spirit… be still my soul;
Christ will come in and keep us whole.

AMEN

Many blessings in your life always…

Cheryl Lyn Wynn

Revelation 22:16 (KJV)

"...I AM the root and the offspring of David,
and the bright and morning star."

John 3:3 (KJV)

"...Verily, verily, I say unto thee, Except a man be
born again, he cannot see the kingdom of God."

John 3:16 (KJV)

"For God so loved the world, that He gave His only begotten Son, that
whosoever believeth in Him should not perish, but have everlasting life."

Revelation 22:17 (KJV)

"...let him that heareth say, Come. And let him that is athirst come. And whosoever will, let him take the water of life freely."

The end of a beginning...

come.

AMEN